Mental Illness

What to Know and How to Help

AMY SIMPSON

Mental Illness: What to Know & How to Help
Copyright © 2025 Amy Simpson
Published by Aspire Press
An imprint of Tyndale House Ministries
Carol Stream, Illinois
rose-publishing.com

ISBN: 979-8-4005-0010-7

All rights reserved. No part of this book may be reproduced or transmitted in any form or by any means, electronic or mechanical, including photocopying, recording, or by any information storage and retrieval system, without permission in writing from the publisher.

The views and opinions expressed in this book are those of the author(s) and do not necessarily express the views of Tyndale House Ministries or Aspire Press, nor is this book intended to be a substitute for mental health treatment or professional counseling. The information in this resource is intended as a guideline for healthy living. Please consult qualified medical, legal, pastoral, and psychological professionals regarding individual concerns. Tyndale House Ministries and Aspire Press are in no way liable for any content, change of content, or activity for the works listed. Citation of a work does not mean endorsement of all its contents or of other works by the same author.

Scripture quotations are taken from the Holy Bible, New Living Translation, copyright ©1996, 2004, 2015 by Tyndale House Foundation. Used by permission of Tyndale House Publishers, Carol Stream, Illinois 60188. All rights reserved.

Cover image: Max4e Photo/Shutterstock.com.

Other images used under license from Shutterstock.com.

Printed in the United States of America
January 2025, 1st Printing

Contents

INTRODUCTION
One Family's Story 5

CHAPTER 1
Mental Illness: An Overview 13

CHAPTER 2
Families in Crisis 31

CHAPTER 3
Misunderstandings about Mental Illness............ 49

CHAPTER 4
How to Help 63

AFTERWORD
Seeing beyond the Illness 91

Resources 97

Introduction

One Family's Story

Some time ago, a woman in her sixties arrived at a shelter for abused women. I'll call her Donna. Donna was accompanied by a younger woman who referred to herself as something like "Moonchild." This was a name she had given herself when she had dedicated herself to paganism and witchcraft. At the shelter, the older woman, Donna, told the staff that she was there because she needed protection from her family who was trying to hurt her and who regularly abused her. So the staff assisted her in filing a protection order against her husband. They asked if she had a safe place to stay, and she told them she was staying with her friend Moonchild. The staff then encouraged Donna to call her husband and tell him that she was somewhere safe, and he shouldn't try to find her. So she left her husband a message without saying where she was, and then she and Moonchild walked out of the shelter.

Moonchild and her boyfriend had met Donna through their occult group. They had told Donna that she had unusual gifts that seemed to give her special insight and make her rituals especially powerful. Donna, they believed, saw things that the rest of them didn't. They encouraged her to explore her unusual gifts further. Donna told them that her family had a very different perspective on her insight. She claimed that her family was cruel and abusive to her; they had told Donna that she had a mental illness, not special gifts, and they tried to get her to take medications. Moonchild and her boyfriend had wanted to help rescue Donna from this terrible situation, so they took her in, and Moonchild and Donna went to the shelter to file the protection order.

After a couple of weeks at Moonchild's place, Donna's family tracked her down. They started calling Moonchild, even though they'd never met her. They told her that Donna was sick and needed medication.

They said that Donna might need to go to the hospital, and they asked her to tell them where they could find Donna. But Moonchild refused to tell them where Donna was, saying that she was protecting Donna from the abuse that her family had inflicted on her.

Not long after the phone calls, things changed. Moonchild and her boyfriend realized that Donna didn't actually make a very good roommate. They suspected there was something wrong with her after all, and they didn't want her to live with them any longer. So they kicked her out of their house, and Donna found herself on the streets.

Donna wandered the city, unsure how to get around and with no idea of where to go. Fortunately, she came across some kind strangers who helped her find a homeless shelter. Donna settled in at the shelter where she received food and a place to stay. But because Donna had trouble following the shelter's rules, which she felt were completely unreasonable and didn't make sense to her, she was told to leave, and once again she was on the streets.

Donna made her way to another shelter, just as the holiday season was arriving. On Thanksgiving Day, a family showed up at the shelter to serve meals. As they were passing out meals, they were shocked to see someone they knew among the residents. It was Donna! The last time they had seen her was many years before, and at that time, they knew her as a quiet and kind pastor's wife, busy raising her four children. They were really confused. Why was Donna living in a homeless shelter? Eventually, as they talked to others about the experience, the information made its way to Donna's family, who learned where these old friends had seen her.

As soon as Donna's daughter heard the news, she traveled to the shelter to find her mother, but by the time she arrived, Donna was gone. Again, Donna had been told to leave because she couldn't follow the shelter rules.

Donna found a third shelter, and it was there that she started exhibiting symptoms of a serious physical health problem. She was taken to an emergency room. When she arrived at the hospital, the personnel quickly realized that this was not a woman simply with a physical problem and without a home, but this was a patient suffering from severe psychosis. Donna was almost completely unaware of reality. She called herself by various names, and she showed many clear symptoms of psychotic illness.

Donna wouldn't consent to be hospitalized but did agree to take part in an outpatient treatment program. One day, when Donna arrived at the treatment center, she surprised everyone by presenting an insurance card. With this information in hand, the hospital was able to determine who she was and bill her insurance company for the services they had been providing. The insurance company sent a statement to Donna's husband, and Donna's family was finally able locate the shelter where Donna was staying.

Over time, both the hospital and shelter realized that much of what Donna had said about her family had been fabricated. Her family was not abusive at all. They loved Donna, they cared for her, and they had called every hospital and shelter in the city for months, looking for her. They had driven the streets. They had talked to social workers and the police—anyone they thought could help them find her. Donna had an extensive history of mental illness. She had been diagnosed with schizophrenia and had received treatment for it for many years. Her paranoia had made her fear her family and caused her to believe in delusions about them and about her life. Because shelters and hospitals must protect the privacy of the people who come to them for help, no one had been able to release information to Donna's family about where she was. For too long, she had disappeared into a system designed to protect people who really are in danger from abusive family members. Unfortunately, Donna's illness made her vulnerable to danger no matter where she was, and all the more so because she was cut off from her family.

With a protection order still in place against Donna's husband, the responsibility fell to one of Donna's daughters, who, in the midst of raising four children of her own, put her life on hold and went to help her mother. When Donna's daughter arrived at the shelter, Donna didn't know who her daughter was. She didn't even know who *she* was. Donna didn't know she was living in a homeless shelter. She thought she was living in a processing center for angels coming and going on assignment from God. Donna had completely forgotten that she had four grown kids and twelve grandchildren. She thought her husband was dead. But Donna did have a family, and that family still loved her and wanted her back again. This reunion with her daughter was only the beginning of a very long journey for Donna—a journey back to her home and family and eventually back to effective mental health treatment and stability.

As you may have already guessed, this story is about my own family. And although Donna isn't her real name,

Donna is my mother. This story describes just one of the many crises in her life and in that of our family.

I want you to know that behind every person with mental illness is a family that has been changed, perhaps even devastated, by the effects of that illness. The reverberations of mental illness go way beyond the individual. People with mental illness may be overwhelmed by depression, anxiety, fear, or even terror. They may have compulsions that control their lives or have thoughts of suicide or self-harm; they may be unable to cope with the simple tasks of everyday life; they may even hear voices or experience hallucinations that redefine reality for them. This is an extremely difficult situation for the person with mental illness and for their family. All of this can feel overwhelming to their loved ones. It certainly was (and sometimes still is) for my family. I know what it's like to walk the long and difficult path of caring for a loved one with mental illness.

If you're a church leader, a ministry volunteer, a coworker, a neighbor, or a friend who wants to know what you can do to help, I am grateful you are reading this book. I hope you find in it the understanding you seek and the encouragement you need to reach out with compassion—the kind of compassion that motivated you to pick up this book in the first place.

If you're a family member of a person with mental illness and you feel like the situation is spiraling out of control and you're not sure what to do, I hope you see in the pages ahead that you're not alone. Help is available. There *are* things that you can do to make a difference for your loved one. And always remember, it's okay to make mistakes along the way, it's okay to admit you can't do it all, and it's okay to ask for help. And it's always okay—and very much welcome— to pour out your heart to your heavenly Father. As 1 Peter 5:7 tells us, "Give all your worries and cares to God"—that's all your frustrations, all your tears, all your anger, all your helplessness, and all your grief. And why? "[Because] he cares about you."

Chapter 1

Mental Illness: An Overview

MENTAL ILLNESS RARELY FITS THE STEREOTYPES. Most people with a mental illness look just like everybody else. It can be easy to think that mental health problems happen only to those on the fringes of society, as if it's something that won't touch our families as long as we just make healthy choices, raise our kids the right way, or go to the right churches and read our Bibles enough. But the truth is mental illness affects far more lives than most of us realize.

How Common Is Mental Illness?

Most people have no idea how widespread mental illnesses are across all parts of society. Let's look at some numbers.

- Mental disorders are one of the leading causes of disability throughout most of the world, including in North America.[1]

- Mental illness in the US is more common than diabetes, heart disease, cancer, HIV, and AIDS combined. When we consider the amount of time, funding, and resources put toward these other diseases compared to what's put toward mental illness, there is quite a disparity.

- Serious and chronic mental illnesses—such as major depression, schizophrenia, bipolar disorder, obsessive-compulsive disorder, panic disorder, post-traumatic stress disorder (PTSD), and borderline personality disorder—are present among 5.5% of the US population, or 1 in 18 adults.[2]

Children and teens are affected by mental illness too. Mental illnesses have been called "the chronic diseases of the young," because the onset of a mental illness tends to occur in a person's youth.[3]

- Half of all lifetime cases of mental illness begin by age 14, and three quarters begin by age 24. Mood disorders often begin in late adolescence and substance abuse in the early 20s.[4]

Our faith communities are not exempt from this either. In the US, the number one frontline mental health resource is the church.

- Church is the most common place that people who seek help for mental illness go to first. Research shows that 25% of people who have sought treatment or some kind of help for mental illness have gone first to a member of the clergy; 16% have gone first to a general medical doctor; 16% to a psychiatrist, and the percentages go down from there.[5]

- One survey across four Protestant denominations found that 27% of families in these churches were directly affected by mental illness.[6]

- Another study found that approximately 30% of Christians with mental illness experienced a negative interaction with the church, such as feeling abandoned or being told that their mental illness was caused by demons or by their sins.[7]

MENTAL ILLNESS BY THE NUMBERS[8]

1 out of 5 US adults experience mental illness.

Church is the most common place people who seek help for mental illness go to first.

11% of US adults with mental illness have no insurance coverage.

1 in 18 adults experience serious and chronic mental illness.

Most Common Types of Mental Illness:

1. Anxiety Disorders
2. Depression and Other Mood Disorders
3. Attention-Deficit/Hyperactivity Disorder (ADHD)
4. Personality Disorders
5. Eating Disorders
6. Schizophrenia and Other Psychotic Disorders

Half of all lifetime cases of mental illness begin by age 14.

Three quarters have begun by age 24.

32 The number of hours caregivers of adults with a mental disorder spend each week on unpaid caregiving.

Duration of Caregiving

Less than 6 months	8%
6 months to 1 year	20%
1 to 4 years	19%
5 to 9 years	17%
10 years or more	33%
Unknown	4%

If you're part of a Christian community, consider this as a missional opportunity. God has brought to your church doors people who are seekers. They are asking questions and looking for answers. They are coming to you because they believe you have love, hope, and faith-based answers for them. They believe you can assure them of God's love. They believe you will be willing to help. And they may believe that you can point them toward some measure of healing in Christ. Unfortunately, they're often met—at a highly vulnerable time in their lives—with something very different.

With so many opportunities to help those in need, how can we respond? I think it begins with gaining a better understanding of this highly misunderstood and misinterpreted illness.

What Are the Different Types of Mental Illness?

Mental illness encompasses a wide range of mental health disorders. While schizophrenia (which my mother has) and other psychotic disorders (the kind we often see sensationalized in movies) are arguably the most severe form of mental illness, they are actually the least common—though still very real. The most common type of mental illnesses are anxiety disorders, followed by depression and other mood disorders. Mental illness symptoms can range from mild to severe, with some mental illnesses always classified as severe by definition. And while some mental illnesses can be episodic (limited in duration), others are chronic (occurring over a person's lifetime).

Anxiety Disorders

A certain amount of anxiety is typical for all of us, especially when we're going through a stressful situation. But what makes anxiety a disorder is when a person experiences anxiety to a degree that it consistently interferes with their daily functioning. Their anxiety, in other words, is in excess—often severely so.

A person's feelings of anxiety may or may not be tied to a specific source of fear, worry, or stress. The individual may experience anxiety symptoms to an extreme degree or over many months or years. Sometimes anxiety is expressed in very disruptive ways: obsessive thoughts, compulsive actions, flashbacks to traumatic events, sleeplessness, intense and paralyzing fear, or an overall sense of dread.

Specific anxiety disorders include agoraphobia, generalized anxiety disorder, obsessive-compulsive disorder, panic disorder, post-traumatic stress disorder (PTSD), social anxiety disorder, and specific phobias.

Anxiety disorders are among the most common form of mental illness. Within a given year, 19% of adults in the US experience an anxiety disorder of some kind. Over the course of a lifetime, 31% of adults will experience an anxiety disorder.[9]

Depression and Other Mood Disorders

Depression and other mood disorders are more than the typical feelings of sadness, grief, and anger that we all go through at times. They are serious emotional disturbances that impair daily functioning. People with mood disorders experience periods of depression that can be severely debilitating. Some people will also go through a period of extremely elevated emotions, a state called mania.

Mood disorders may make it very difficult for a person to go to sleep, get out of bed, interact with others, concentrate, or fulfill basic responsibilities at home, school, or work. Those with mood disorders may lose their appetite and get headaches, stomachaches, or joint pain. They often feel overwhelmed by negative thoughts, even thoughts of suicide. It can be quite a challenge for people with depression to get the mental health treatment they need, because their depression may be so severe that they lack the energy or decision-making resources to ask for help, and their feelings of worthlessness can lead them to believe they don't deserve help in the first place.

Mood disorders are complex, and they are sometimes caused by imbalances in brain chemicals, but often by many other factors. They may be genetically inherited and triggered by circumstances, especially stress, grief, and trauma. Specific mood disorders include depression, bipolar disorder, dysthymic disorder, and major depressive disorder.

In any given year, 9.7% of adults in the US experience a mood disorder. Of these, 45% are considered severe. Among adolescents, 14% experience a mood disorder each year. The bulk of these cases are considered severe, affecting 11% of those between ages 13 and 18.[10]

Attention-Deficit/Hyperactivity Disorder (ADHD)

People with ADHD have difficulty focusing their attention, maintaining that focus, and shifting focus from one thing to another. ADHD is a neurologically based disorder, but its exact cause is still unknown. Those with ADHD become easily distracted and have difficulty maintaining a long attention span. They also may exhibit hyperactivity (overactivity) and have trouble controlling their impulses and behavior.

Because ADHD symptoms usually begin before age seven, it's commonly diagnosed in children. But it's not only a childhood disorder; ADHD can continue through adolescence and adulthood.

The three different types of ADHD are (1) hyperactive-impulsive, (2) inattentive, and (3) inattention combined with hyperactivity and/or being impulsive.

Of adults in the US, 4% live with ADHD. Nearly 9% of 13- to 18-year-olds experience ADHD. Among children, ADHD is one of the most commonly diagnosed disorders.[11]

Personality Disorders

Personality disorders are named so because these illnesses are, in a sense, woven into an individual's personality. These disorders are not episodic; they're pervasive. They don't just come and go during one's lifetime, nor are they limited to only one or two relationships. Instead, they're expressed over a long period of time (often in patterns) in how a person makes decisions, engages in relationships, and views the world around them. People with personality disorders have a distorted perception of themselves and others.

Personality disorders are difficult to recognize because people with these disorders seem "normal" to themselves. In fact, they often perceive the people around them as abnormal or highly flawed. Such individuals may have serious trouble keeping a job, developing stable relationships, and coping with ordinary stressful situations; but they typically blame others for these problems. It's important to keep in mind that a personality disorder diagnosis should

only be done by a mental health professional. We want to be careful not to make assumptions or label someone as having a personality disorder just because they seem odd, are outside the cultural norm, or are struggling with employment and relationships.

Specific personality disorders include antisocial personality disorder, avoidant personality disorder, borderline personality disorder, histrionic personality disorder, narcissistic personality disorder, and paranoid personality disorder. In any given year, 9% of adults in the US are living with some kind of personality disorder.[12]

Eating Disorders

An eating disorder affects a person's relationship with food and body image in a very harmful way. This is not merely a case of bad eating habits, occasional overindulgence, or fad dieting. Eating disorders involve severe disturbances to emotions, perceptions, and behaviors; and without proper treatment, they can be life threatening.

Eating disorders cause extreme overeating or undereating. Overeating is typically followed by one of two things: (1) purging through vomiting, using laxatives, fasting, or exercising excessively; or

(2) weight gain and intense emotional distress over the consequences of overeating, which can in turn lead to more overeating. The disorder anorexia nervosa is characterized by extreme undereating. People with anorexia nervosa truly view themselves as overweight, even when they are physically wasting away.

People with eating disorders commonly experience other mental illnesses too, such as depression and anxiety. Specific eating disorders include anorexia nervosa, bulimia nervosa, and binge-eating disorder.

Anorexia nervosa affects 0.6% of adults in the US, with bulimia nervosa affecting 1% over the course of a lifetime. Binge-eating disorders affect 2.8% of adults in the US over the course of a lifetime, and 1.2% in a given year. Among adolescents, 2.7% develop some kind of eating disorder.[13]

Schizophrenia and Other Psychotic Disorders

Psychotic disorders are the least common type of mental illness, but they are among the most severe. These disorders disrupt a person's perceptions of reality. Of the psychotic disorders, schizophrenia is by far the most common.

People with psychotic disorders may not be able to distinguish between what's real and what's not real, or what's occurring now and what took place in the past. They may also have a very hard time showing emotions or showing them accurately and appropriately. They often act in a very disorganized way, saying and doing things that others can't understand. Psychotic disorders are characterized by delusions (false beliefs) and hallucinations (false perceptions). A person's delusions may make them believe that they're in danger, either from a specific perceived threat or a more general sense of fear. Their hallucinations may come in the form of hearing voices and seeing people or things that aren't there.

Psychotic disorders are often sensationalized in movies and on TV, which unfortunately leads many to assume that people with psychotic disorders are beyond help. But these disorders are treatable—though getting proper treatment and maintaining that treatment can be quite difficult. For a variety of reasons, over half of those with schizophrenia do not receive the care they need.

Specific psychotic disorders include brief psychotic disorder, delusional disorder, schizoaffective disorder, and schizophrenia.

Schizophrenia and related psychotic disorders affect an estimated 0.25% to 0.64% of the US adult population.[14] Schizophrenia is the most common of the psychotic disorders; it's unclear how prevalent the others are.

A WORD ABOUT AUTISM

Autism Spectrum Disorder (ASD) is the name for a group of developmental disorders of the brain that fall along a spectrum of severity and symptoms. These symptoms impair social functioning, communication, and typical emotional responses.

ASD is not a mental illness, but it is closely linked to mental health problems for a few reasons:

- People with ASD develop mental health disorders—such as depression or an anxiety disorder, like obsessive-compulsive—at a higher rate than the general population.

- ASD is included in the *Diagnostic and Statistical Manual of Mental Disorders* (DSM) and is often diagnosed by mental health professionals.

- Symptoms of ASD, like those of mental illness, often affect the emotional and social realms of life.

- ASD is often treated using the same types of interventions that are used for mental illnesses, such as medication and therapy.

- Individuals and families affected by ASD struggle in many of the same ways as those affected by mental illness.

So ASD is in a different category but is included here because of these similarities.

People with ASD don't express emotions the way most people do, and they have difficulty communicating that goes far beyond mere shyness or awkwardness. They often make little eye contact, don't seem to notice other people who are trying to talk with them, and have trouble understanding social cues. They sometimes use language in a limited way or in a way that only family members and others who know them well can understand.

They may also engage in repetitive behaviors, like moving their fingers or arms in the same way over and over, walking in specific patterns, or repeating the same words or phrases.

ASD symptoms usually begin in early childhood, with most diagnoses made before the age of eight. While the exact causes are not known, ASD seems to be influenced by a variety of genetic and environmental factors, especially during development in the womb.

About 2.8% of eight-year-old children in the US have autism spectrum disorder. It's nearly four times more common in males than in females.[15]

Several specific disorders—such as Asperger's disorder (Asperger syndrome), childhood disintegrative disorder (CDD), and Rett's disorder (Rett syndrome)—that were once regarded as distinct are now all considered to be on the autism spectrum.

Chapter 2
Families in Crisis

My mother's illness began many years ago when she was much younger, as schizophrenia typically does. The onset of schizophrenia usually happens in a person's late teens to early adulthood, and that's when it began for Mom.

When I was a young child, I always saw my mom as fragile. In our home, my siblings and I sensed that she was unable to seriously help or protect us. Instead, it seemed that she needed our help and our protection. Growing up, I didn't know that she had something called schizophrenia—and I wouldn't have even known what that word meant if I had heard it.

Both of my parents were able to keep her illness hidden for many years, although the effects of it were sometimes obvious. Eventually, though, hiding her illness became impossible. When I was in my early teens, her schizophrenia became very pronounced. It turned our lives upside down. She had been experiencing psychotic episodes for many years before that, but now she suffered her first fully incapacitating psychotic break, and she was never able to entirely recover from it. Although she had not been healthy for decades, her disorder had now grown to the point that it made her completely unable to discern and understand reality for a period of time. Although it would take us years to really comprehend what had happened to her, we sensed that life would never be the same. And that reality became more apparent with time.

Over the decades that followed, we walked with her through a string of run-ins with the harsh effects of her disease. These included difficult and broken relationships, paranoid fear, hospitalizations, public embarrassment, religious confusion, occult activities, homelessness, danger, worry, sleepless nights, arrests, jail, and even prison time. Periods of stability and hope were followed by slow or sometimes sudden losses of the person we knew and loved. Battles with shame and stigma kept us quiet and isolated, even from each other, for far too long. We tried our best to fight for the life and well-being of a woman we cherished, who still had a purpose and a place in this world. Often our family was left out of the loop of information—out of the circle of medical care—floundering as we tried to figure out how to help Mom, and also how to deal with our own overwhelming emotions at the same time.

For too many years, my family did not seek much sympathy or support from the people around us. We knew—and the culture around us reinforced what we "knew"—that we were not supposed to talk about mental illness. We got the message that we were alone, we were worthy of shame, and we were supposed to

pretend everything was fine; and we were somehow supposed to keep it all under control. So that's what we tried to do. For a long time, we thought we were alone.

When mental illness makes its way into a family, that family is thrown into crisis, even when the illness is mild or short-term. The loved one with the illness needs a lot of care, and this tends to monopolize the family's resources. The person might be incapable of earning a living and seem unmotivated or unwilling to do anything productive. They might be very difficult to deal with, becoming demanding and behaving selfishly, erratically, frighteningly, and even violently. Such behaviors can make it extremely difficult or even impossible for family members who love them to live with them. And these same difficulties are true even for family members who don't live with them.

- People who are caring for an adult loved one affected by mental or emotional health problems spend an average of 32 hours per week on caregiving.[16]

- People with mental illness are far more likely than the general population to experience problems like unemployment, cardiovascular and metabolic diseases, substance use disorders, homelessness, difficulties in school, and dropping out of high school. Each year, people with serious mental illness are incarcerated in jails about 2 million times. Some are jailed repeatedly.[17]

All these effects of mental illness have a profoundly negative impact on families, friends, and communities. If you are walking this challenging journey of caring for a loved one with a mental illness, you'll probably recognize very well the following five things that families experience. If you're not on such a journey but want to help a family in the middle of a crisis, understanding these five things will provide you some insight about what they are facing.

1. Confusion

No one becomes an expert in navigating a mental health crisis—or the intricacies and frustrations of the mental health care system—until they need to. And because it's such a stressful experience, people who are caught up in the challenges of a mental health crisis are among the least equipped to handle everything that will come their way. Families routinely find themselves in the dark. They're unsure how to get the help they need for their loved one and themselves.

Our mental healthcare system is badly broken and hard to navigate. It can be very challenging to get access to care. What do you do when you need an adjustment in your loved one's medication, but the psychiatrist is booked for the next six weeks? What do you do when you find out the insurance didn't cover the hospital stay, leaving your family with a huge bill? What do you do when no one will tell you what your loved one has been diagnosed with or what their medications are for?

Historically, doctors have been reluctant to diagnose mental illness because of the stigma associated with it and because insurance companies have been quick to discriminate against people with mental health problems. These challenges are improving as legislation has forced insurance companies to offer benefits for mental health problems that are on par with other types of health problems, but insurance companies still pressure hospitals and doctors to shorten treatment. Those short hospitalizations tend to focus only on stabilization, instead of setting people up for long-term success. The average length of a hospital stay for psychiatric care is about seven days, but the average time that it takes for a psychiatric medication to work is anywhere from two to six weeks. So when people with a mental illness go into the hospital and leave a few days later with a prescription in hand, they usually have no idea whether that medication is going to work for them. And if it doesn't, they find themselves hospitalized all over again.

These hospitalizations—especially forced hospital stays—are traumatizing for everyone involved; and those who are repeatedly hospitalized are sometimes labeled as "frequent fliers" and treated like annoyances to the system or like hopeless cases. In fact, most would be far less likely to make repeat trips to the hospital if they were provided with adequate care with some longer-term consistency, rather than given a very short course of treatment and released to the care of confused and traumatized loved ones.

Privacy laws exist for a reason: to protect individuals and their right to be free from intrusion into their personal lives. But for families trying to take care of someone with a severe mental illness, these laws often work directly against their best efforts to get help for their loved one. If the person with the mental illness doesn't sign a consent form for healthcare workers to talk with their family, then family members may have no idea what's going on; families are kept out of the loop, like my family was. Families are forced to rely on their loved one for information, even when that person may not be able adequately to describe their medical treatment or even what their diagnosis is. This sort of situation has improved in recent years as the system now provides for mental health professionals to interact with a designated caregiver and makes allowances for caregivers to be appointed, even if the patient is incapacitated. But this can still be a serious challenge in a moment of crisis.

In a severe crisis, police officers become frontline mental health workers by default. They're the only ones who have the power to get an individual to medical care when nobody else can—and even members of law enforcement can only do that under certain strict conditions. The police officers who show up during a mental health crisis may or may not be well equipped to deal with such a situation, putting families in the difficult place of trying to explain a very complicated story about what's really going on with their loved one. As we have seen in news headlines in recent years, sometimes these encounters are fraught with misunderstandings and can turn disastrous, even fatal.

To add to the confusion, family members are often in shock and traumatized by the experience of seeing a loved one exhibit symptoms of mental illness. They may lose their sense that there is any kind of predictable future beyond the present moment, and they may fear that their current crisis represents a new normal, all the while wondering how they can possibly cope with it. It's scary to look ahead and see an unknown or overwhelming future. Family members may need therapy themselves, and they certainly need support from caring individuals. But many people have no idea where to turn for this kind of help and may be too overwhelmed by a loved one's needs to even begin to think about their own needs.

2. Exhaustion and Depletion of Resources

Caring for a person with a mental illness, no matter how much you love them, can be exhausting. When mental illness hits a family, it takes its toll.

Because the symptoms of many chronic mental illnesses tend to repeat in cycles, family members spend a lot of time and energy being hyper-vigilant. They try to anticipate when the next crisis is coming. They watch for signs that a loved one is losing their grip on reality, retreating into a dark place, or engaging in self-harm. They monitor medications to see if their loved one is really taking them. They try to contain and minimize disruptive behavior. Sometimes they just try to get the person out of bed for a while, to get them to eat anything at all, or to keep them from dying by suicide.

Navigating the requirements of insurance companies and advocating for loved ones in the healthcare and legal systems can be a full-time job. And when a family member is hospitalized, visits take a lot of time and scheduling.

Lost work, expensive medications, hospitalizations, residential care, and alternative schooling can cause large financial burdens. One single mother I know had to sell her house and take out $100,000 in loans to pay for her daughter's one-year stay at a residential school. She would say this was well worth all the money because it saved her daughter's life, literally. But her family is now deeply in debt, and that's something they will deal with for years to come. Other friends have had to devote the bulk of their resources to helping one child in crisis and then seeing the heartbreaking long-term consequences in their other children's lives as they have dealt with the experience of feeling lost and unsupported.

Mental illness also changes a family's dynamics. It can be easy to fall into unhealthy patterns. Family members sometimes suppress their own personalities, opinions, and needs in an effort to keep the person with mental illness stable and happy. In my home growing up, this meant we kept our feelings hidden and didn't invite our friends over or introduce them to our parents. It also meant following bizarre rules that Mom would create for our home but couldn't explain.

As with other illnesses, the person with the mental illness requires much of the family's resources, often with little left for those who are well. This can mean a disruption to employment situations, school attendance, child care, and other routine commitments for the rest of the family. Deprived of what they need, family members will adapt the best they can, but they also may come to resent the person with the illness. This is just one of the many reasons why family members in the midst of a loved one's mental health crisis need to seek help for themselves also (more on how to do this later).

3. Grief

Mental illness is a thief. It takes from suffering people a piece of who they are. It robs families of life-giving, reciprocal relationships with someone they need and love, leaving families with a deep sadness over their new reality. I feel this loss every day. Some days it's more acute than others. Mother's Day is tough, especially sitting through church sermons that idealize mothers' roles in our lives.

I've had many conversations with people who also feel this kind of loss. One man said this of his experience of sitting in church with his son who has bipolar disorder: "The church has divorce groups, grief groups. Well, in some ways what we're dealing with here is divorce, is grief, and yet the kid's sitting right next to me."[18]

This is a serious loss—the kind that redefines life as we know it. Family members need to grieve the loss of the relationship they had or the one they always hoped to have with the person with chronic mental illness. For families affected by a long-term serious illness, this grief is always fresh, never totally behind them. Every time the ill loved one suffers a relapse, drains the family emotionally, creates a public spectacle, can't get out of bed, mentally disengages due to medication, goes to jail or the hospital, or is absent for holiday meals and celebrations, family members suffer. They grieve.

These emotional wounds are conditions that God can use in our lives, but they are excruciating to endure. No one just "gets over" this kind of grief. The only remedy is redemption through God's grace, which provides a healing much different and far greater than "getting over" it.

4. Spiritual Struggles

Watching a loved one suffer from an ongoing mental illness challenges our faith, no matter how deeply rooted that faith is. Sometimes that struggle uproots our faith altogether. For both the person with the illness and their family, this can be a confusing spiritual crisis. People wonder why God isn't relieving the suffering. They question if maybe they did something bad to deserve this. They experience anger and disappointment with God. And if they turn to their church for help and receive judgment and bad advice instead of compassion and assistance, that's a painful spiritual wound to bear.

For a person suffering from delusions, loss of faith may be part of the mental illness itself. The person may not be able to discern truth from lies or know how to seek spiritual help from those who have their best interest at heart, instead of from people who will take advantage of them.

Satan certainly will use any opportunity to lead a person away from faith in Christ—as he did with my mother. When she began to go astray and embrace the occult, it was after decades of following Christ and participating in church life. She has since rejected occultic beliefs and returned to faith in Christ. In her own words, this is what it was like back when she started having delusions during church services:

> I thought I had some special insights. There were hidden meanings in what I was hearing in church. It seemed that the truth which I had believed for so long was no longer accurate. Because of the secret information I was receiving in my thinking, I began to think, "I just don't believe this way anymore." … My medication was not working properly for at least two to three years. I didn't realize that, and my family didn't either. I never said anything to anyone about the secret messages I was supposedly getting. These were delusions. But I thought they were spiritual gifts and the Lord had drawn me close. I remained that way in our evangelical church for two full years before leaving the church.[19]

At this time of crisis, Mom came across people who themselves were spiritually deceived and who were all too eager to help her walk away from the church and into spiritual darkness. Her spiritual crisis became my family's as well. We wrestled with our own spiritual questions—the kind of hard questions that never seem to get discussed in Sunday school.

For those whose faith bends but doesn't break, wrestling through troubling questions can build faith stronger. And that's true even if we don't get clear and satisfactory answers to our questions. People need support through this process. Struggling with spiritual questions in the context of a supportive church—where faith is deep and honest enough to acknowledge that we live in a sinful and broken world

and that some questions don't have answers this side of heaven—can make a huge difference in whether our questions destroy or develop our faith.

Churches where this kind of growth can happen tend to be churches where influential people (whether in formal leadership roles or not) are exercising the courage to embrace a truly biblical faith—one that does not need to believe the world is better than it is, a faith that leaves no room for spiritual self-reliance or achievement. When we can acknowledge that we really are all broken and in desperate need of a Savior, we start the journey toward building a safer place to suffer. But we can't stop there. We must also embrace the reality that we do have a Savior who is more than capable of entering into our pain, redeeming our suffering, and ultimately healing all of creation. Our answers are in Christ, and we have every reason to confidently proclaim that he offers hope and ultimate healing, even if we don't find ourselves medically healed now.

There are practical steps we can take to welcome truly supportive conversations and actions (see chapter 4), but spiritual safety begins with our theology and our willingness to live by faith.

5. Shame and Stigma

Besides the mental illness itself, many people say the greatest source of suffering is the stigma that comes with the illness. Shame too often keeps people from seeking care, talking about their problems, and understanding how common mental illness really is.

I grew up going to church. In fact, my dad was a pastor for about a decade. We were very involved "church people." But in all my years sitting in those pews, I never heard a sermon that mentioned mental illness. No one addressed it in Sunday school or youth group. I had the distinct impression that church was not a place where I could ask the questions that I most needed to ask about what was happening to my mom. Why was my "good Christian family" suffering this way? Why didn't God fix it?

Our faith communities can be full of well-intentioned people who let misunderstanding and stigma keep them from reaching out and ministering to suffering families. In that sense, unfortunately, my story is not unique. I have had conversations with hundreds of people who have stories similar to mine.

Many secular spaces aren't any better. Pop culture tends to treat the mentally ill as jokes, terrifying criminals, or subhumans. Society often judges and blames people for developing disorders of the mind. The truth is no one chooses to have a mental illness. Yet we shun people with mental disorders, laugh at them, and accept their sense of shame as if it were warranted. Their families get the message too: keep your home life a secret.

These feelings of shame are reinforced if, when they reach out for support or confide in others, people keep their distance or react in insensitive ways. I suspect that underlying a lot of the poor reactions to people with mental illness are some false assumptions and bad theology that all need a thorough reexamination.

Chapter 3

Misunderstandings about Mental Illness

IF WE WANT TO BE THE KIND OF PEOPLE, CHURCHES, and communities who respond with compassion and dignity toward those with mental illness and their families—who really see them as precious human beings made in the image of God just as much as you and I are—then we need to start rethinking some popular assumptions. There are three common misunderstandings about mental illness that are particularly damaging.

MISUNDERSTANDING #1: **Mental illness isn't real.**

Some people think that mental illnesses are not real medical—or even psychological—conditions.

"Depression is just normal grief."

"Eating disorders are teenagers acting out."

"ADHD is made up."

"Anxiety means you're not trusting God enough."

Perhaps you've heard people say things like this. Perhaps you've said them yourself. But the truth is mental illness is real, and it must be taken seriously.

Some people assume that mental illness simply reflects a spiritual problem, not an actual illness. Of course, we would never tolerate such a dismissal of other kinds of illnesses, like cancer or diabetes. Well, brain injuries, chemical imbalances, and disorders of the mind should also not be dismissed. They are just as real as other illnesses. They're documentable, and they're treatable.

We are horrified (and rightly so) by people whose religious beliefs cause them to deny medical treatment to the sick, yet some people claim mental illness should not be treated because such treatments are not found in the Bible. The Bible does not describe the use of chemotherapy, painkillers, antibiotics, or general anesthesia either, yet those treatments have helped millions of suffering people.

Denying the reality of mental illness in our faith communities has the same effect as denying the reality of other illnesses. It hinders people from crying out in their pain, bringing their illness to Jesus, and finding the help they need to ease their suffering and find wholeness. It forces sick people and their families to choose between their church's teachings and their own life and health.

It doesn't have to be this way.

I like how Dwight L. Carlson explains this in his excellent book *Why Do Christians Shoot Their Wounded?*

> Most people consider it appropriate to call a roofer when the roof leaks, a plumber when the sink won't drain, or a tow truck when a car won't start. Though God could miraculously solve each of these problems, in most instances he doesn't. It has nothing to do with his ability or his sufficiency for the task. He is able to,

but he chooses not to use that means. Rather, his sufficiency enables me to deal with these problems and get whatever help is needed to solve them. There is no question that God is ultimately sufficient.[20]

Did you catch that? Believing that mental illness is real and that it needs professional treatment *doesn't* mean that God is not in the picture; nor does it mean that a person isn't relying on God as they seek help. In fact, there's a lot of research that shows that spiritual practices like praying, belonging to a church, and reading Scripture are very supportive to one's mental health. It's just that these alone don't provide all the treatment that people with acute mental illness need. Many people also need medical help, and sometimes getting that treatment is a matter of life and death.

When we discourage people from pursuing necessary treatment because of some kind of spiritual reason, we take a great risk with them and their lives.

MISUNDERSTANDING #2: Christians can't have mental illnesses.

All sorts of places—workplaces, charities, churches, social clubs—have official rules and policies they operate by. But have you noticed how it's often the unspoken "rules" that are the most influential? In some faith communities, one unspoken rule is that no messes are allowed through the church doors—or at least not the kind of crippling, persistent messes that a few more prayers and more Bible reading can't cure. In these spaces, people suffering from the "mess" of mental illness are given the impression that that's just not something real Christians have to deal with. A friend observed, "One of the things I learned from therapy is there is nothing you need to be afraid to talk about, but that's not the faith system that a lot of churches promote." Another expressed it this way: "People think Christians aren't supposed to get depressed, because they're supposed to be joyful."[21] An overemphasis on victorious, joyful Christian living can leave little space for people to grapple with and talk about the very real and very painful reality of suffering.

It's true that, as Christians, we *do* have victory in Christ Jesus. In fact, that's the heart of the gospel. Consider what the apostle Paul says:

> But thank God! He gives us victory over sin and death through our Lord Jesus Christ. (1 Corinthians 15:57)

> I can do everything through Christ, who gives me strength. (Philippians 4:13)

> Despite all these things, overwhelming victory is ours through Christ, who loved us. (Romans 8:37)

God has promised to remove us from this world someday and to replace these imperfect bodies with new bodies (including, I believe, new brains) perfectly suited for life in a world without decay and suffering (see 1 Corinthians 15:12–57). In the meantime, however, life on this side of heaven is far from perfect. We're all broken and flawed. The Bible clearly tells us that our bodies, minds, and souls are impacted by sin, sickness, and decay, and we should not expect *complete* victory in this present life. We are all affected by the world around us and the brokenness within us. This, too, is Christian doctrine at its most basic. But we sometimes forget to walk in the humility of the knowledge that we're all scarred, broken, and will face many sorrows. We forget the "not yet" part of "already and not yet."

Jesus said:

> I have told you all this so that you may have peace in me. Here on earth you will have many trials and sorrows. But take heart, because I have overcome the world. (John 16:33)

Peter wrote to suffering believers:

> Dear friends, don't be surprised at the fiery trials you are going through, as if something strange were happening to you. Instead, be very glad—for these trials make you partners with Christ in his suffering, so that you will have the wonderful joy of seeing his glory when it is revealed to all the world. (1 Peter 4:12–13)

We are not immune to suffering from illnesses—and that includes mental illnesses. We are affected as much as anyone else by the curse on this fallen world. There's no reason for us to assume that people who trust in God, follow Christ, and repent of their sin won't have the trouble that is part of the human experience in this world. Those who are truly effective in ministering to others in need are the ones who are aware of the need in themselves. If you're approaching others as though "You have problems, and I don't," then you won't be a safe person for people to turn to.

When we don't make space for the truth that people in our faith communities can and do suffer from illnesses that affect the brain, then, on top of the initial crisis of dealing with a mental illness, we set them up for a secondary crisis. We send them the unspoken message that their mental health problems must mean that they're not real Christians, that they don't belong here, or that God has walked away from them. Nothing could be further from the truth.

Christ does redeem our suffering, and one day he will make us new, with new bodies that don't decay, minds that don't get sick, and spirits that don't lose heart. We have great hope in this life and for the next, but our hope is not in the avoidance of suffering in the here and now.

> All creation is waiting eagerly for that future day when God will reveal who his children really are. Against its will, all creation was subjected to God's curse. But with eager hope, the creation looks forward to the day when it will join God's children in glorious freedom from death and decay. (Romans 8:19–21)

Christians live in the light of this future hope, even while walking in a shadowy world where sin and pain are present. Only when we embrace both these aspects of life on earth can we help bring lifesaving hope to hurting people.

MISUNDERSTANDING #3: The person with the mental illness must be to blame.

Some people believe that mental illness is essentially a spiritual problem that can be fixed by the sufferer through spiritual means. Perhaps because brain disorders affect an individual's cognitive abilities and emotional processing and because this in turn affects a person's behaviors and spiritual expression, there is a lot of confusion about what causes mental illness. Some people believe it's caused by demon possession or demonic attack. Others think it's caused by a lack of faith. Some see the root cause as unconfessed sin. As one woman put it, "The first thing about church was, if you've got a problem, you must not be walking with the Lord." Another woman, who had depression and sought counseling, was told by her pastor that she must have undealt-with sin in her life that was making her depressed.[22]

Individuals with mental illness and their families often feel condemned for what they're experiencing. And sometimes when they go to their church leaders, instead of finding the no-condemnation grace of Jesus, they find an assumption that they must have done something wrong to deserve their suffering. It's sometimes even implied that they'd better fix themselves and their family's problems if they want to be part of the faith community.

Spiritualizing mental illness translates into blaming sick people for their illness. This kind of thinking traps people in working harder and harder to achieve enough righteousness to make themselves well. This is not the gospel message. It's a message that discourages people from acknowledging their mental health struggles and from seeking help.

I'm not saying that this means our physical self and spiritual self are somehow independent of each other. I believe our minds, bodies, and spirits are in fact more interrelated than we can understand. Just as physical pain affects our spirits, spiritual problems can lead to problems in our brains and bodies. Reckless and sinful behaviors can have a devastating impact on a person's mental health. But this fact doesn't justify the assumption that all mental illnesses lead back to an individual's spiritual failures. We must guard against being like Job's friends in the Bible, who, when they saw a suffering person, reacted by accusing Job of causing his own problems. Nor do we want to make assumptions like Jesus's disciples who, when they encountered a man with blindness, immediately asked, "Why was this man born blind? Was it because of his own sins or his parents' sins?" (John 9:2). Listen to Jesus's reply: "It was not because of his sins or his parents' sins…. This happened so the power of God could be seen in him" (John 9:3). Then Jesus, the Great Healer, restored the man's sight, and the man went forth as a living testimony to the miraculous power of God.

Mental illness can happen to any of us. If you pay attention, you can find countless examples of faithful people whose families have been affected by mental illness. Many are pastors or missionaries. Some have been the most highly admired Christians in history.

Mental illness strikes all kinds of people, and being a Christian will not ensure that mental illness doesn't strike you or your family.

Over the decades, I have struggled with many spiritual questions about my mom's illness. Why did God allow my mom—the one who prayed with me and taught me about Jesus—to suffer from a mental illness that regressed her own spiritual maturity? Why didn't God answer my prayers to miraculously heal her from it all? Why didn't he protect her from all the dangers she encountered as an extremely vulnerable person? Today, I still don't have all the answers to these questions. But what I do know is that throughout my family's journey with our mother, God has given us several powerful reminders of his presence with her and with us. God has shown us that even when her illness pulled her away from him, he never abandoned her. No one is beyond God's reach.

Mental illness doesn't mean that God doesn't love you or that you haven't done enough for him. We live in a world that's deeply and pervasively damaged by rebellion against God. Good behavior and serving God are not magical charms that will make our problems go away. We don't hold the remedy for our infirmity; Christ does. But he has not fully unleashed his healing upon the world. God loves every single one of us and he grieves with us in our suffering. The apostle Paul assures us in Romans 8:35–38 that having trouble— even the very worst kind of trouble—does not mean God's love has left us:

> Can anything ever separate us from Christ's love? Does it mean he no longer loves us if we have trouble or calamity, or are persecuted, or hungry, or destitute, or in danger, or threatened with death?... No, despite all these things, overwhelming victory is ours through Christ, who loved us. And I am convinced that nothing can ever separate us from God's love. Neither death nor life, neither angels nor demons, neither our fears for today nor our worries about tomorrow—not even the powers of hell can separate us from God's love.

And I would add to that list: *not even mental illness.*

Chapter 4
How to Help

WHETHER WE KNOW IT OR NOT, WE'RE SURROUNDED by people who are dealing with mental illnesses and by families who are trying their best to care for them. These families and their loved ones need the assistance of caring communities who are not too scared to talk about mental illness, too impatient to stick with them, or too weary to help them, again and again.

If you're a leader in any kind of ministry, you're actually on the front lines of mental health care. As mentioned earlier, clergy is the number one place people go to first to seek help for mental health problems. Your response to individuals and families reaching out for help is tremendously important. The same is true for lay people in the church. People with mental illnesses and their loved ones are a precious part of your community, and how you treat them matters. When those with mental illness and their families are shunned, rejected, abandoned, or ignored by others in the church, those people can feel as if they're being shunned, rejected, abandoned, or ignored by God. This is not the way God responds to us. Jesus welcomes the weary, the struggling—all the heavy-burdened people—and his followers should do the same.

> "Come to me, all of you who are weary and carry heavy burdens, and I will give you rest.... Let me teach you, because I am humble and gentle at heart, and you will find rest for your souls."
>
> MATTHEW 11:28-29

There are plenty of ways we can help people affected by mental illness, whether they're part of our faith community, a neighbor down the street, or a close family member. Some ways require a big investment; others mean simply loving them in small ways. Most are far more practical and doable than many people assume.

Ways to Help

1. Treat people with mental illnesses like people.

We can start by treating people with mental illnesses like *people*. Sounds simple, right? Well, it doesn't always happen.

Some mental illnesses, like my mother's, are more apparent than others. To outsiders these people might seem quite strange. Too often I've walked into a church setting with my mother and noticed people begin to look away and keep their distance—and this was when Mom was lucid and behaving in a normal and predictable way. My mother noticed this too, but sadly, she was used to being treated this way. People with mental illness know when they're being shunned and avoided. These hurtful experiences just compound the pain they already feel.

When we don't understand something or aren't sure what to do with an uncomfortable feeling of awkwardness around someone with a mental illness, our first reaction may be fear. Of course, if the person truly presents a danger, it's always appropriate to call the police or take other action to keep people safe. But if the fear is unfounded, try not to let it overwhelm you. Treat the other person how you would want to be treated. This can be simple: Make eye contact. Smile. Say "Hi." When you encounter someone who has a mental illness and they behave in a way that's a little different from what you might expect or that you don't quite understand, try to see beyond the behavior and really see the *person* inside them. You can show kindness, even as you honor any necessary boundaries.

"Do to others whatever you would like them to do to you. This is the essence of all that is taught in the law and the prophets."

MATTHEW 7:12

2. Be a friend.

When someone confides in us that they're depressed or feeling anxious or that they have some kind of mental disorder, our first thoughts might be: "I don't know what to do. I can't help with that. They need professional help, and I'm not qualified." Well, that person might need professional help, but there's no special qualification required to be their friend.

It's good to refer people with mental illness and their families to qualified counselors, but be careful not to abandon them once they're connected with professional help. This is a huge mistake I've seen some churches make. They think, "If I can just get this person to a counselor, the professionals can take it from there. I've done my job. They're getting help." True, they are getting some help, but they are not getting the kind of help that only a caring community of believers can give them. Psychologists are not there to be their friend. Mental health workers are not there to offer spiritual guidance and spiritual counsel. Support groups are not meant to be the only kind of loving community that surrounds people in need. They need friends. They need a community. They need companions to walk with them on their faith journey.

You can start by being a listening ear. As you develop a friendship with the person and their family, you can speak honestly with them about their experiences, allowing them to open up with you about what's going on. As you build trust in the relationship, you might be able work with their mental health professionals to support their treatment. Just remember, you don't need to feel a burden to "fix" them or "treat" them. That's not your job as a friend. What you *can* do is demonstrate the kind of love God has for all of us—the kind that doesn't waver.

WHAT TO SAY

It can be awkward and tricky to talk with someone or their family about a person's mental health—especially when you don't know what the disorder is or when what's going on is not even acknowledged as a mental health issue. I've found that a good approach is to ask questions, rather than make statements. This creates space for people to open up, if they want to.

- "How are you doing?"
- "How are things at home?"
- "How can I pray for you and your family?"

When they answer, listen closely to the words they use. They may describe specific behaviors or feelings.

- "He won't get out of bed."
- "She's really angry right now."
- "I feel hopeless."

You can use that same language to ask more questions, speak words of support, offer specific help, follow up with the person, pray for them, and perhaps encourage them to seek more assistance.

- "I can see he's having a really hard time."
- "It must be very difficult dealing with her anger."
- "How long have you been feeling so down?"

This type of wording can be far less intimidating than using the language of mental health diagnosis.

If the person seems open to talking more, it's okay to ask whether they have seen a professional. Suggest that they might talk to a pastor, doctor, or counselor. You can offer information about specific resources, like support groups and mental health professionals. This should be done with sensitivity and care. If you have your own experience receiving mental health care, you might offer a bit of your own story. This can go a long way toward making the person feel safe.

3. Offer to help in practical ways.

Mental illness has been called the "no casserole" illness. What do we do when someone is recovering from surgery or grieving the passing of a loved one? We help out. We stop by. We bring casseroles. It doesn't have to be so different when families are dealing with a mental health crisis.

Practical assistance is often an overlooked aspect of helping out. When we focus on the illness itself and think, "I can't fix their mental problems or alleviate their emotional suffering," we feel helpless. We throw our hands up in the mistaken belief that there's nothing we can do to make a difference.

Because there are many ways people struggle during a mental health crisis, there are actually many ways we can help. Most of them involve providing very practical support: physical, financial, social, and spiritual. These are the same kinds of things we do to help people in other types of crises. This is not mysterious, and it's a great place to start.

You can bring meals. Give rides to the grocery store—or buy them groceries. Take them to the doctor. Provide childcare. Take their kids to school. Ask them how they're doing. Visit them in the hospital. If finances are tight, you can help with gift cards to purchase gas, prescribed medications, or other household necessities so they don't have to choose between treatment and basic family needs. Encourage them to keep taking their medications. Tell families who are pursuing health—who are getting help or seeking help—that you admire their choices to care for themselves and their loved one. A little piece of encouragement may go a long way in helping them to keep at it. Offering your assistance might seem simple, even cliché, but it takes courage. It takes following through on what you offer. It takes commitment and patience, and it may require you to hang in there for the long haul.

It's also important to prayerfully consider what you have to offer and to be intentional about offering what you actually can. Be clear and explicit about this. For example, saying "I can give you a ride to the doctor on Thursday" is a clear offer with built-in boundaries. "Whatever you need, just let me know" is an open-ended invitation that should not be given unless you're ready to give whatever the person asks for, if possible. Vague offers with no clear limits may lead to different expectations. You might think you're offering one thing, but the other person might be expecting something quite different. It's also hard for people to accept vague offers if they're reluctant to impose or they lack a sense of what's possible. People in crisis don't always know what they need, nor are they always able to express their needs in a straightforward manner, so it might take some clarification to get a clear picture of what they need and what you can reasonably provide.

4. Have patience.

Helping also requires patience, especially with chronic mental illness. You might have to help a person or a family again and again. That can be very hard, believe me. I know how tough it can be to be in it for the long-haul with someone who has a recurring problem with mental illness. Just because you help someone get healthy or just because you help a family get through a crisis, doesn't mean they're not going to face the same thing next year.

One of the best ways I've found to guard against discouragement and impatience is by having realistic expectations. Understand that a mental health problem may be an ongoing issue. We can't expect people to shake it off. Just as a person can't "will away" a case of diabetes or a broken arm, a person with a case of mental illness can't just get over it or make it go away.

We have had remarkable advances in recent years in brain science, psychology, and medications; and most mental illnesses have actually become highly treatable conditions, which is great news. Treatments for some mental illnesses are up to 90% effective *when* people get the treatment they need and *when* they stick with the treatment.[23] But that doesn't mean that 90% of people are cured. Treatment doesn't necessarily equal cure.

Think of mental illness as a spectrum of debilitation and chronicity, just like other medical conditions. It might be reasonable to expect someone with a broken arm to fully recover in a few months or so, but it's not reasonable to expect someone with an autoimmune disease to have the disease go away and never come back. Similarly, a case of postpartum depression might resolve itself with a hospital stay, short-term medications, and several visits with a therapist; but schizophrenia and bipolar disorders are another story altogether.

Many mental illnesses are never fully resolved—but they can be managed. Figuring out which medications will work for which individual takes some trial and error. Some medications will be more effective than others. Some won't work at all. And some will cause strange results. Others that were working will stop working. For people who need lifelong mental health treatment, success might mean learning to function well most of the time, despite their illness. For their families, success might mean safety, proper care, and a healthy relationship with their loved one but not necessarily having the person back just like they were before the mental illness hit.

Sometimes treatment isn't enough. Despite the best efforts of loved ones and professionals, fighting mental illness seems at times like a losing battle. (This is true of other forms of severe illness as well.) This doesn't mean that medical treatment and support are illegitimate, and it doesn't mean that we should give up using the best treatments available to help those we can. This should instead challenge us to be more understanding and patient with those who may be dealing with mental health problems for the rest of their lives.

Know that if you help someone and that person still struggles, it doesn't mean that you've failed or that they've failed. And it doesn't mean it wasn't worth helping them. Having this as our mindset will enable us to let go of the impulse to pull away completely when things don't go as planned, fearful that we can't ever give enough or do enough. It doesn't have to be all or nothing.

> "Always be humble and gentle. Be patient with each other, making allowance for each other's faults because of your love."
>
> EPHESIANS 4:2

5. Set healthy boundaries.

Setting healthy boundaries is how you can establish and maintain a balance that's not only good for you but also good for the person and family you're helping. Let me explain.

On one side of the equation, we may fear that loving someone with mental illness or a family affected by mental illness will mean that we'll get sucked into harmful patterns and that their issues will take over our lives. We know we'll need to say *no* sometimes when they ask for something we can't or won't do, but saying *no* can be hard, especially to a person in crisis. So instead of communicating a healthy boundary, we just pull away. We ignore them. We don't show up. We "ghost" them. We might tell ourselves it's because we don't want to be unkind to the other person ("They'll get the message eventually"), but it's usually more of a matter of managing our own discomfort. While saying *no* might feel unkind, it's actually much kinder to do the difficult thing and communicate a boundary with honesty and gentleness, rather than keeping our distance without explanation.

On the other end, we may try to do too much. We think that helping someone and their family means fixing their problems and becoming their sole resource. So we try to be their hero and save them. But when we do that, we rob them of the opportunity to find other resources, both external to themselves and within themselves. We operate with a lack of faith that God can and will provide additional resources. We may reinforce an unhealthy idea that they aren't capable of turning to outside resources and asking for help. We can end up enabling a sense of helplessness that they need to grow past to have a better life. This is not a sustainable situation. Instead, it's valuable to have a mindset that honors the fact that we are not the complete answer to anyone else's problems. There are things we can do to help each other, but we can't make each other's mental and emotional struggles go away. A hero complex is a ticket to heartbreak, frustration, and burnout. And a "fixing them" mentality will make the other person feel like a project.

So what do healthy boundaries actually look like?

Even though someone is struggling with a mental illness, you should still maintain standards of morality and respectful behavior toward others in your church or community. Overlooking a person's inappropriate, harmful, or abusive behaviors toward others—or toward you—is destructive. And it does no favors to individuals with mental illness either. They need healthy people around them to give them objective feedback. If the person is part of a group— for example, a Bible study group—the group leader should communicate agreed-upon expectations openly and lovingly to all members in the group and then hold to those standards consistently. Help the person with mental illness pursue and maintain health by insisting on a healthy community around them.

It's also okay to put boundaries around your personal information. You don't have to provide your address, phone number, or other information, even if someone asks for it. If you don't feel comfortable with what they're asking for, offer another way to communicate: "Here's my email address; I check it every day," or "I'll see you at small group each week."

If you're helping out in practical ways—bringing over groceries or giving them rides, for instance—this may require sharing some contact information and going to their house. If you're unsure about the safety of a situation, it's good practice to bring someone else with you when you visit—someone who can handle the person with sensitivity and care. But if at any time

you suspect that the person may present a danger to themselves or to you or others, it's always right to call 911 or have others help you take the person to a hospital. That's not a situation to handle on your own.

As you're helping out, if you reach a point where you recognize you're in over your head, acknowledge your limitations and encourage the person to receive more capable care elsewhere. This doesn't mean abandoning the friendship and practical support you can provide. But it might mean modeling resourcefulness and doing some research to point them in a helpful direction. You might also need to reevaluate and redraw your boundaries—and that's okay. Exercise good boundaries that honor your limitations.

5 Ways to Help

1. Treat people with mental illnesses like people.
2. Be a friend.
3. Offer to help in practical ways.
4. Have patience.
5. Set healthy boundaries.

For Family Members

A mental illness crisis may be leaving you and your family feeling overwhelmed. I know it can be extremely difficult to navigate medications, therapy, insurance, and housing. Hospitalizations can be impossibly expensive, and dealing with the repeating cycle of symptoms means putting your life on hold again and again. Adjusting to the chronic nature of some illnesses may mean letting go of cherished dreams.

And then there's the stigma. Shame about your loved one's mental illness can keep you suffering in silence and walking this difficult journey alone. It doesn't have to be this way. I'd like to share four things you can do to change this.

1. Get healthier.

In airplane safety demonstrations, flight attendants always tell passengers, "If the oxygen masks come down, put on your mask first, before helping someone else with theirs." Why yours first? Because you aren't able to adequately help someone else if you can't breathe yourself. The same principle applies when caring for a loved one with mental illness. If you're not taking care of your own well-being, you will not be able to offer effective care and support for your family member.

Do the work that it takes to become a healthier individual—and a healthier family too. If you need counseling, seek counseling. If you were raised by someone who has a severe mental illness, you've probably got some stuff to work through as an adult. Be willing to take a look at toxic patterns within your family—things like codependency—that might actually be preventing all of you from getting healthier.

The path to healthy relationships means you're going to have to acknowledge the reality of your loved one's mental illness. You can't sweep a mental health problem under the rug, hoping it'll go away. It won't. You will need to talk about it honestly with your other family members and the safe people in your life. This can be difficult because mental illness may be stigmatized even within your own family. Do some family members mock the person with mental illness? Do they tell them to just get over it? Are they too ashamed to even admit there's a mental health crisis? You can set the example by seeking support for yourself, even if others or the person in your family with an illness will not. Doing so helps break the stigma. There's no shame in needing and getting help.

Though it can be challenging to find the right kind of help that will work best for you and your family, it's always worth the effort. There are many good resources available for families, and you can start by looking through the list of resources at the end of this book.

2. Reach out for help.

Telling others that your family needs help will feel risky. You're likely in a vulnerable emotional state, and you probably don't have the capacity to deal with the misunderstandings or bad advice you'll get in return. So it's important to start with people you believe will respond to you with compassion and care. Begin with those you think are most likely to be kind to you and will want to help—even if you're not sure that they know how to help. If you know of someone who has walked a similar road, reach out to them, even if you don't know them well. People who have been on this journey may be more likely to help, and they may become your best resources.

If someone asks you how they can help, tell them what you need. Be specific. I know it's hard when you're in the middle of a crisis and you feel like you need mountains of help, but you don't have a clue what anybody can do about it. So think about practical needs. Do you need rides for your loved one? Meals? Do you need help filling out paperwork or researching options for how to pay for expensive medications? Do you need somebody to sit with a family member so you can run errands? Think about your spiritual needs, too. Do you need someone to pray with? Someone to talk to about your faith questions that have come up because of this mental illness? Think about your social needs. Do you need someone to sit with you—just to listen to you or be silent with you? Do you need a small group of people who will let you be honest about your struggles or maybe a church-based support group for people who are going through similar hardships? Think through what it is that you actually need and what others can offer. Instead of ruminating, "I wish my church would help" or "I wish so-and-so would do something," let them know specifically how they can help. Many people will understand and be willing to help, but you

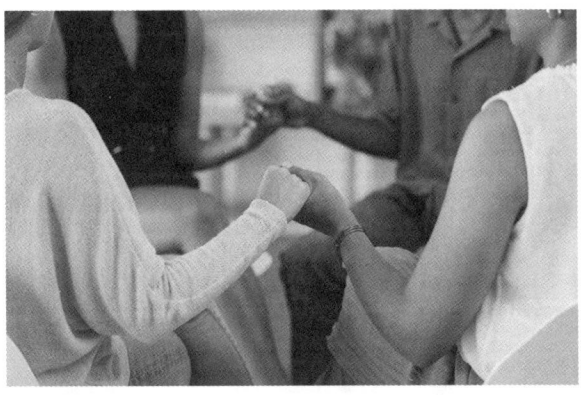

won't find those people or that help unless you make yourself known. Suffering in silence causes its own kind of destruction. You need other people to love you and lift you up.

When you start asking for help, be aware that not everyone is going to respond as you would hope. Don't blame them or lash out at them for not getting it. We often don't understand things we haven't experienced, so try to speak in a way that other people can hear and will respond to positively, rather than attack them for not meeting your needs or understanding your situation. If you don't get an honest or loving response, and it's clear they really don't want to help, don't push it. It's not worth the energy. Look elsewhere for help. Find people and places that will be supportive of you and your family on this journey.

3. Educate yourself.

Learn as much as you can about your family member's specific mental illnesses (if known) and any medical and community resources available. Two good national resources for this are the National Alliance on Mental Illness (nami.org) and the National Institute of Mental Health (nimh.nih.gov). Both have fantastic websites with information that's easy to understand for those of us who are not mental health professionals. Helplines are available too; for example, the Substance Abuse and Mental Health Services Administration helpline is 1-800-662-HELP. You can also dial 211 in the US to find out about local services available in your area. (See the list in the back of this book for more resources.)

When your loved one is receiving mental health care, don't be afraid to ask the people who are treating them questions—lots of them. Ask questions of their doctors, nurses, counselors, and/or social workers. These people might not be able to give you all the information you're looking for—or might not give you the answers you hope for—but I encourage you not to give up. Keep fighting for the information you

need. Keep looking for the most effective medical care available.

And know this: You don't need anyone's approval or permission to advocate for your loved one. If another family member says you're wasting your time or a pastor says that seeing a psychologist is wrong, you don't have to agree. Allow other people to have their opinions, but you do what you believe is best to help your family member who has a mental illness.

4. Tell your story.

Be wise in opening up to people about your story. Some people are not ready to hear about your experience with mental illness. Some people will not understand. I encourage you to pray that God will send compassionate people your way and that he will give you wisdom about who might be ready to hear your story. If they respond to you in a loving way, that can make you bolder to share with more people.

Before you tell your story to a larger audience, however, think carefully about how to talk about it in a way that is healthy, that normalizes the struggle, and that communicates grace and solidarity to others. Spend time in prayer asking God to give you the wisdom you need. Believe that God may use the power of your voice to comfort people who feel rejected, marginalized, and frightened into silence, who wonder if God has turned his back on them. You can testify to God's faithful care. You can communicate to others that they aren't the only ones walking through this kind of hardship, and you can help strike a blow against stigma and shame, which keep us separated from one another when we desperately need to be connected.

Let me offer a word of caution, though: I believe sharing your story is best done when you're not in the throes of an acute crisis and only after you have received ministry and care from others and have had some opportunity to heal and make sense of your experience. Even if the story is ongoing, it will be helpful to others only if you're able to share it in a way that others can enter into it and receive it as ministry. If you're actively bleeding (emotionally speaking), others will simply feel the need to stop your bleeding. But if you're sharing your story behind your scars, they will feel safe to enter into your story and receive something for themselves.

It's also important that you don't share other people's stories if they don't want them told. If your family members consent to your sharing about your family's story, you can do so freely. But if some are not comfortable with you telling their story, share only what is yours to share and what parts of their story you have permission to share. Remember, you have your own story; you don't have to give the details of other people's illnesses or experiences. You can share about your own situation, even without identifying the person in your life with mental illness. This may mean your story will be vague or very short on detail, but that's okay; it's still worth sharing.

4 recommendations for family members

 1. Get healthier.

 2. Reach out for help.

 3. Educate yourself.

 4. Tell your story.

Afterword

Seeing beyond the Illness

I'm happy to say that God's power and grace have prevailed in my mom's life. While she still lives with schizophrenia and the effects of it, she did renounce her involvement in the occult and has come back to faith in Christ. Medication is helping her find stability and she's making healthy choices for herself. Our family has learned to come together quickly in times of crisis, communicate directly and courageously, and collaborate to advocate for Mom's needs—and care for ourselves in the process.

One Christmas, I received a package from my mom in the mail. When I opened it, I found outfits that she had sewn for my kids. They were custom-made to fit my children exactly. They were beautifully and lovingly crafted. I'll admit, there were long stretches of years, decades even, when I would have told you that she would never have the capacity to do a project like that—or even have the interest in doing it. But she has surprised me in the best ways.

My mother's mental illness is not gone, and I can't say she'll never have another psychotic episode—in fact, I'm pretty sure she probably will. But I can say that she is the picture of the kind of hope that all people with mental illness have. Modern medicine offers great possibilities for the treatment of many mental illnesses. Loving and consistent friendships are the very best context for encouraging people to get and maintain treatment. For families, finding acceptance and support from others can make all the difference. And even more powerful is God's love, grace, and redemption through our struggles.

Over the years, my mother has lived in several long-term care facilities. These places were able to provide the kind of safety and treatment that she needed and a level of attention that would not have been possible if she had lived at home. I'm so grateful she has had safe places to land and caring staff to look after her. But this sometimes has been the extent of my vision for her: safety, stability, treatment.

God has a bigger vision for her.

Once when I visited her at a facility, she was excited to introduce me to some of the people she had met there. A staff member told me about the tremendous influence that my mom had had on the other residents. He recognized the presence of Christ in my mom's life. Because of her, he said the other residents had more hope and joy in their lives. Because of her, people felt listened to; they felt like they had a friend. "Your mom," he said, "does this for people."

My mom has also told me about a friend she made, another resident at her assisted living facility. Her friend is not a believer in Jesus, but he is very intrigued by the book she is reading and journaling through. You see, my mom has an *Inspire* Bible, a creative journaling Bible, that's very special to her. She loves spending time in that Bible and moving at her own pace to understand and absorb the Word of God. She adds her own creative responses—coloring the words of Scripture, drawing, tracing—helping her concentrate and reflect on what she reads. Whenever anybody in my family talks with her, she tells them about the progress she's made reading it and creatively expressing her responses—down to the very page and verse number. Her curious friend stops by every day to see what kind of progress she's made in this Bible since the day before. On a daily basis, my mom is sharing bits of God's love as she shows off her favorite book.

These are the moments when I realize that God has a much bigger vision for my mom in these places than I sometimes can see. Despite whatever debilitating mental state my mom had been in when she arrived at these different facilities, God still used my mom for good at each place.

I hope you take heart and find encouragement in knowing that mental illness does not make anyone marginal to God. He's in the business of redemption. Regardless of how we may see people with mental illness, he sees every single person for who they are. He loves us all more than we can imagine. In God's grace, we can extend that same kind of love toward one another. We can see each other through the eyes of God's Spirit who helps us recognize the value and potential in one another.

Regardless of our mental health, we are all equally valuable in God's eyes, and all of Christ's followers have a place and a purpose in his kingdom. God has a purpose for everyone, and our limitations don't limit him. People with mental illness are precious to him and they should be precious to the rest of us.

Resources

Books

The Anxiety Reset: A Life-Changing Approach to Overcoming Fear, Stress, Worry, Panic Attacks, OCD and More by Gregory L. Jantz, PhD, with Keith Wall (Tyndale House Publishers, 2021). This book helps readers understand and work through a plan to improve their mental health by addressing triggers in their lifestyle and thought patterns.

Anxious: Choosing Faith in a World of Worry by Amy Simpson (InterVarsity Press, 2014). This book acknowledges both the helpful and the destructive power of anxiety in our lives and encourages readers to move away from a life of worry in favor of faith.

The Anxious Christian: Can God Use Your Anxiety for Good? by Rhett Smith (Moody Publishers, 2015). In this book the author helps readers understand how God can use anxiety in our lives to produce spiritual growth.

Beyond the Clinical Hour: How Counselors Can Partner with the Church to Address the Mental Health Crisis by James N. Sells, Amy Trout, and Heather C. Sells (InterVarsity Press, 2024). This book presents a challenge to churches and their leaders—and a model to follow—to recognize their place in the system of care for mental health issues, fill a gap that only the church is equipped to fill, and minister to hurting people in the name of Jesus.

Companions in the Darkness: Seven Saints Who Struggled with Depression and Doubt by Diana Gruver (InterVarsity Press, 2020). This is a collection of personal stories and lessons from seven well-known Christian leaders from history, all of whom acknowledged their struggles with depression in the midst of lives of faith.

Darkness Is My Only Companion: A Christian Response to Mental Illness by Kathryn Greene-McCreight (Brazos Press, 2006). An episcopal priest and college professor shares her theological perspective on mental illness along with stories from her own experience with bipolar disorder.

Diagnostic and Statistical Manual of Mental Disorders, 5th ed. text rev. (DSM-5-TR) (American Psychiatric Association, 2013). This weighty professional manual is used by mental health professionals for reference and diagnosis.

Grace for the Afflicted: A Clinical and Biblical Perspective on Mental Illness by Matthew S. Stanford, PhD (Biblica Publishing, 2008). This book presents detailed information about various types of disorders, with biblical perspective on each.

Grace for the Children: Finding Hope in the Midst of Child and Adolescent Mental Illness by Matthew S. Stanford, PhD (InterVarsity Press, 2019). This book helps church leaders and other Christians understand and minister to people affected by common mental health disorders in childhood and adolescence, the stages of life when most cases of mental illness begin.

Grieving a Suicide: A Loved One's Search for Comfort, Answers, and Hope, rev. and exp. ed., by Albert Y. Hsu (InterVarsity Press, 2017). Based on the author's own painful story, this book serves as a useful guide for grief and moving forward in the wake of losing a loved one to suicide.

LifeCare by Solome Skaff (Muddy Pearl, 2019). In this resource the author walks readers through a process toward healing and seeing their painful stories redeemed through relationship with Christ.

Many Forms of Madness: A Family's Struggle with Mental Illness and the Mental Health System by Rosemary Radford Ruether with David Ruether (Fortress Press, 2010). A Berkeley professor discusses the history of treatment for mental illness and describes her own family's experience in caring for her son with schizophrenia.

Mental Disorders and Spiritual Healing: Teachings from the Early Christian East by Jean-Claude Larchet (Sophia Perennis, 2005). Translated from French, this work provides an exploration of ancient Christian theology in relationship to mental illness.

Mental Health and the Church: A Ministry Handbook for Including Children and Adults with ADHD, Anxiety, Mood Disorders, and Other Common Mental Health Conditions by Stephen Grcevich, MD (Zondervan, 2018). This book offers a helpful professional perspective on what is and is not helpful for individuals and families affected by mental health issues. The author lays out a plan for how churches can effectively include people living with these challenges, along with advice for family members who want to support spiritual growth in their loved ones with mental illness.

A Parent's Guide series—These concise books equip parents to understand, relate to, and communicate with their teenage children. These booklets cover a variety of topics from a Christian perspective, including several related to mental health: *Suicide and Self-harm Prevention; Mental and Sexual Health; Walking through Grief; Depression and Anxiety; Eating Disorders; Body Positivity*; and more. Find them at axis.org or tyndale.com.

Resurrecting the Person: Friendship and the Care of People with Mental Health Problems by John Swinton (Abingdon Press, 2000). A university professor and former mental health chaplain explores the importance of friendship as a foundational model for ministry to people with mental illness.

Surviving Suicide Loss: Making Your Way Beyond the Ruins by Rita A. Schulte, LPC (Northfield Publishing, 2021). The author speaks as a counselor and a loved one who lost her husband to suicide. She offers a guide for understanding and moving beyond the profound grief that follows this devastating kind of loss.

Troubled Minds: Mental Illness and the Church's Mission by Amy Simpson (InterVarsity Press, 2013). In this book, Amy Simpson shares many stories from people affected by mental health problems, including her own family. She gives insight into the needs of people in crisis and the experiences they often encounter in churches, and she calls the church to respond by living its mission as the people of God.

When Life Goes Dark: Finding Hope in the Midst of Depression by Richard Winter (InterVarsity Press, 2012). The author, a psychiatrist, offers both a medical and a theological perspective on depression, along with insights into how to live with depression as a Christian and move toward healing.

When Your Family Is Living with a Mental Illness by Marcia Lund (Augsburg Books, 2002). This small booklet, part of the Difficult Times series, is a resource for loved ones who need support, referrals to other resources, and assurance that they are not alone.

Why Do Christians Shoot Their Wounded?: Helping (Not Hurting) Those with Emotional Difficulties by Dwight L. Carlson, MD, (InterVarsity Press, 1994). This book points out that we often condemn hurting people for their pain, challenges us to better, and helps equip churches to effectively care for wounded people.

Podcasts and Videos

Fresh Hope for Mental Health—This podcast features interviews with experts and people who discuss their experiences with mental health challenges. It places a strong focus on hope and redemption through Christ and loving support (freshhope.us/resources/fresh-hope-for-mental-health-podcast).

Key Ministry—This podcast is about issues related to both mental health and disability. It's especially focused on how we can make church more accessible to individuals and families who live with these challenges (keyministry.org/podcast).

Meier Clinics—This podcast covers a variety of topics related to mental health from a Christian counseling perspective (mentalhealthnewsradionetwork.com/our-shows/meier-clinics-podcast).

The Mental Illness Education Project—This organization produces video projects designed to educate, destigmatize mental illness, and advocate for better services (miepvideos.org).

Shadow Voices: Finding Hope in Mental Illness, directed by Burton Buller (Mennonite Media Productions, 2005)—This video features stories of people living with mental illness, along with interviews with mental health experts and clergy; it's available on DVD and on YouTube (youtube.com/watch?v=aEzo05BrlCY).

National Organizations and Websites

Alcoholics Anonymous—This fellowship of recovery and support groups is for people with alcohol addictions (aa.org).

American Association of Christian Counselors—This membership association website features a "Find a Christian Counselor" tool to help you find a credentialed Christian counselor in your area (www.aacc.net).

Anxiety and Depression Association of America—This association provides information, support, and advocacy for people affected by anxiety disorders and depression (adaa.org).

Children and Adults with Attention-Deficit/Hyperactivity Disorder (CHADD)—This nonprofit organization provides information and support to individuals and families affected by ADHD (chadd.org).

Hope for Mental Health—This resource, associated with Rick and Kay Warren and Saddleback Church, is designed to offer Christ-centered support and networking for individuals and churches (https://hope4mentalhealth.com).

Narcotics Anonymous—This fellowship of recovery and support groups is for people with drug addictions (na.org).

National Alliance on Mental Illness (NAMI)—"America's largest grassroots mental health organization dedicated to improving the lives of individuals and families affected by mental illness," NAMI provides information, advocacy, support groups, referrals, and more; while not a Christian organization, NAMI exists in part to provide the kind of support that families, churches, and their leaders need (nami.org).

National Eating Disorders Association—This association provides support and access to care for individuals and families affected by eating disorders (nationaleatingdisorders.org).

National Institute of Mental Health (NIMH)—This federal government agency's site is easy to navigate and packed with information about mental health and specific mental disorders, mental health research, and links to more resources (nimh.nih.gov/index.shtml).

Substance Abuse and Mental Health Services Administration (SAMHSA)—A division of the US Department of Health and Human Services, this organization's site provides information and links to a variety of resources (samhsa.gov).

Wellness Recovery Action Plan (WRAP)—This website is the gateway for people with mental illness to develop a Wellness Recovery Action Plan, a personalized plan that encourages them to take responsibility for their recovery and sustained health (mentalhealthrecovery.com).

XXX Church—An online Christian-based resource to help people overcome addiction to pornography (xxxchurch.com).

For Churches and Ministry Leaders

Anchor International—This organization helps churches develop peer-support programs for mental health (anchorinternational.org).

Church Mental Health Summit—This virtual event features a variety of presenters who speak on topics related to mental health, the church, and faith (churchmentalhealthsummit.com).

Fresh Hope for Mental Health—This Christian organization provides hope through Christ-centered peer support groups for individuals affected by mental health problems, as well as their loved ones (freshhope.us).

Hope Made Strong—Hope Made Strong equips church leaders to connect with each other and to build sustainable care ministries (hopemadestrong.org).

Key Ministry—Focused on both disability and mental health challenges, Key Ministry advocates for churches to become more accessible and welcoming to affected individuals and families (keyministry.org).

Mental Health First Aid—This course from the National Council for Mental Wellbeing trains individuals and organizations to better understand mental health-related diagnoses and symptoms and to act as first responders in moments of crisis (mentalhealthfirstaid.org).

Mental Health Grace Alliance—This nonprofit organization reminds us that recover from mental illness is possible. They offer multiple resources to support Christ-centered mental health recovery and ongoing wellness (mentalhealthgracealliance.org).

Spiritual First Aid—This course trains and certifies churches and other faith-based organizations to serve as "spiritual first responders and mental health champions" (spiritualfirstaid.org).

Stephen Ministries—This longstanding organization trains and equips church leaders and laypeople to effectively minister to hurting people of all kinds within their churches (stephenministries.org).

Hotlines

211:
Dialing 211 provides callers with information and referrals to services in their local community, including mental health-related support.

National Domestic Violence Hotline:
thehotline.org or call 800-799-SAFE (7233).

National Mental Health Hotline:
mentalhealthhotline.org or call 866-903-3787.

Suicide and Crisis Line:
988lifeline.org or call, text, or chat 988.

Notes

1 Mayo Clinic, "Mental Illness": www.mayoclinic.org/diseases-conditions/mental-illness/symptoms-causes/syc-20374968; John Hopkins, "Mental Health Disorder Statistics": www.hopkinsmedicine.org/health/wellness-and-prevention/mental-health-disorder-statistics#.

2 National Institute of Mental Health (NIMH), "Mental Illness": www.nimh.nih.gov/health/statistics/mental-illness.

3 As quoted in "Psychiatric Epidemiology: It's Not Just about Counting Anymore," by Thomas R. Insel and Wayne S. Fenton, *Archives of General Psychiatry,* 2005;62 (6): 590–592.

4 Ronald C. Kessler et al., "Lifetime Prevalence and Age-of-Onset Distributions of DSM-IV Disorders in the National Comorbidity Survey Replication," *Archives of General Psychiatry,* 2005 Jun; 62 (6): 593–602.

5 Philip S. Wang, Patricia A. Berglund, and Ronald C. Kessler, "Patterns and Correlates of Contacting Clergy for Mental Disorders in the United States," *Health Services Research*, 2003 Apr; 38 (2): 647–673.

6 Edward B. Rogers, Matthew Stanford, and Diana R. Garland, "The Effects of Mental Illness on Families within Faith Communities," *Mental Health, Religion and Culture*, 15 (3): 301–313.

7   Matthew S. Stanford, "Demon or Disorder: A Survey of Attitudes toward Mental Illness in the Christian Church," *Mental Health, Religion and Culture*, 10 (5): 445–449.

8   Statistics can be found in: NAMI www.nami.org/about111mental-illness/mental-health-by-the-numbers/#theripple-effect-of-mental-illness, www.nimh.nih.gov/health/statistics/mental-illness, "On Pins and Needles: Caregivers of Adults with Mental Illness" (2016) https://www.nami.org/wp-content/uploads/2023/07/B-5-Findings-from-a-National-Survey-of-Family-Caregivers-of-Adults-with-Mental-Illness.pdf; Mental Health America, "Access to Care 2022," https://mhanational.org/issues/2022/mental-health-america-access-care-data#:~:text=11.1%25%20(over%205.5%20million),a%20mental%20illness%20remain%20uninsured; Kessler, "Lifetime Prevalence"; Wang, "Patterns and Correlates".

9   NIMH, "Any Anxiety Disorder": www.nimh.nih.gov/health/statistics/any-anxiety-disorder.

10 NIMH, "Any Mood Disorder": www.nimh.nih.gov/health/statistics/any-mood-disorder.

11 NIMH, "Attention-Deficit/Hyperactivity Disorder (ADHD)": www.nimh.nih.gov/health/statistics/attention-deficit-hyperactivity-disorder-adhd.

12 NIMH, "Personality Disorders": www.nimh.nih.gov/health/statistics/personality-disorders.

13 NIMH, "Eating Disorders": www.nimh.nih.gov/health/statistics/eating-disorders.

14 NIMH, "Schizophrenia": www.nimh.nih.gov/health/statistics/schizophrenia.

15 NIMH, "Autism Spectrum Disorder (ASD)": www.nimh.nih.gov/health/statistics/autism-spectrum-disorder-asd.

16 National Alliance on Mental Illness (NAMI), "Mental Health by the Numbers": www.nami.org/about-mental-illness/mental-health-by-the-numbers/#the-ripple-effect-of-mental-illness.

17 NAMI, "Mental Health by the Numbers": www.nami.org/about-mental-illness/mental-health-by-the-numbers/#the-ripple-effect-of-mental-illness.

18 Amy Simpson, *Troubled Minds: Mental Illness and the Church's Mission* (IVP Books, 2013), 74.

19 Simpson, *Troubled Minds*, 78–79.

20 Dwight L. Carson, *Why Do Christians Shoot Their Wounded? Helping (Not Hurting) Those with Emotional Difficulties* (InterVarsity Press, 1994), 35.

21 Simpson, *Troubled Minds*, 148–149.

22 Simpson, *Troubled Minds*, 107.

23 NAMI, "Facts about Mental Health": https://namica.org/what-is-mental-illness/#section-facts-about-mental-health.

Hope and Healing

Unmasking Emotional Abuse

Six Steps to Reduce Stress

Ten Tips for Parenting the Smartphone Generation

Five Keys to Dealing with Depression

Seven Answers for Anxiety

Five Keys to Raising Boys

Freedom From Shame

Five Keys to Health and Healing

When a Loved One Is Addicted

Social Media and Depression

Rebuilding Trust after Betrayal

How to Deal with Toxic People

The Power of Connection

Why Failure Is Never Final

Find Your Purpose in Life

Here Today, Ghosted Tomorrow

Caregiving

Forgiveness

Mental Illness

Secure

rose-publishing.com